Make Each Moment A Memory

Vol. I

By Deanna Anderson

You must live in the present, launch yourself on every wave, find your eternity in each moment.

Henry David Thoreau

#MAKEEACHMOMENT

ISBN-13: 978-1547193073
ISBN-10: 1547193077

Manufactured in America as a print-on-demand by CreateSpace Independent Publishing Platform

Concept and Design rights belong to Deanna Anderson. Cover designed by Deanna Anderson using Canva.com.

CreateSpace, USA
www.createspace.com

#MakeEachMoment

Dedicated to...

All the selfie sticks, scrapbook albums, front-facing cameras, free food samples, besties, travel buddies, travel brochures, collectibles & memorabilia, postcards, T-shirts, vendors, free stuff, photo stick props, friends and families that help Make Each Moment A Memory....

Make Each Moment A Memory

A guide on how to make the most of each moment in life.

Vol. I

Table of Contents

Introduction

People often tell me that I do a lot—and perhaps I do, but I think it is more than that. I think its more of knowing how to make the most of each moment, of each thing that I do.

I try to appreciate each moment whether it is a small event, like a movie premiere, or a big event, like an annual vacation. I plan for that one thing days or even weeks beforehand.

If it is a movie, I might purchase the book or graphic novel, or buy the T-shirt. If it is an event, I collect the free promo notices or gear. If it is a new business, I collect the business card. If it is a place, I buy a souvenir. If it is a concert, movie, or play, I keep the ticket stubs.

And I take a lot of pictures. A lot.

Years ago, in my teens and early 20's, I collected business cards, ticket stubs, and other mementos of places I had gone and stuck them in an album—one of those 'old-fashioned' kind with the sticky pages and the vellum cover sheets.

When my husband and I were dating, each time we went to a unique store or ate at a sit-down restaurant we would collect a business card, tear it in two and each keep half (21 years later we still have these).

I had gotten out of this habit of collecting mementos like these for several years, and it is only recently that I have started back up.

Now I scrapbook photos of special occasions or

events. Along stickers or embellishments, I might add a business card, the ticket stub, or some other memento.

I also take pictures, and by having a camera phone, I don't miss a photo opportunity. As soon as I got my first smart phone with front-facing camera, my new favorite pastime became taking selfies.

I upload photos to Facebook in individual albums, and I print a few select ones to scrapbook.

Then, at the tail end of last year I thought, "wow, I do a lot...I wonder how many things I did this year?" and that inspired me to start the blog *A Mile in My Shoes* (@theresnothingtodo).

It is part review of the things I do, places I see, and people I meet, and partly to show those "there's nothing to do" people just what all there is to do.

The inspiration for this book came from that blog. In the blog, I started tossing in tips on what I do to make the most of each moment. I realized then, that I wanted to reach a larger audience and make those tips more easily available.

I want others to know how to live in the moment. Life is stressful enough. Do not worry about the future (it will be there when you get home) or regress about the past (it is over and done with).

I want people to have as much fun as I do when I am out somewhere 'adventuring' (as my friend and I have started calling it).

I truly hope that this book helps bring people into the moment and helps them to appreciate and enjoy whatever it is that they are doing.

I would love to hear from readers through my Amazon website at www.amazon.com/author/

deannaanderson, and on my Facebook page @DeannaAndersonAuthor or my blog *A Mile in My Shoes* on Facebook @theresnothingtodo or email me at deanna.anderson.author@gmail.com.

Deanna Anderson

Using This Book

This is a guidebook. Take what works for you and use it. Not every tips needs to be utilized, and certainly not every tip every time.

Read it, remember some of the tips, or highlight the ones that appeal to you.

When an event is coming up, glance through the book and figure out which item(s) you want to do and make a conscious effort to do them.

Eventually making each moment a memory will come as second nature. In the meantime:

Take this book along with you.

Read it, share it, and give it as a gift.

Impart its wisdom to others.

Write it in, book mark it, or highlight your favorite passages or tips.

Take a photo of you with it and share it with me in email or on my Facebook pages.

Use this book; it is yours now.

Read this book

Use some of the tips

Share it

A picture is worth a thousand words

Take a Selfie

Selfies get a bad reputation on social media with posts and articles dedicated to inappropriate or dangerous selfies. It is also a misconception that the selfie taker is vain or conceited.

I love selfies and I see nothing conceited or vain about it. If I had someone else take a photo of me its not vanity, so why is it in a selfie?

In fact, aside from the limited arm's length or selfie stick view, I prefer selfies. I fancy myself a decent photographer, whereas I don't often like photos that others take of me.

Selfies give control back to me—the photographer. I can adjust the tilting of the head or my smile, find just the right lighting or position, and I have control of what is in the background.

Taking selfies is not vain, it is not conceited, and it is not going to be the destruction of society.

In fact, according to *Shape Magazine*, studies show that selfies boost our level of happiness, confidence, and self-worth; and help us to smile more naturally, (like practicing before a mirror).

However, there is some social etiquette to taking a selfie.

Do not take selfies in highly sensitive places or situations: funerals, with your comatose great-uncle behind you, within the ruins of a concentration camp.

Be aware of the surroundings and background. We have all seen the 'selfies before disaster struck' with a bear or a speeding train bearing down on the selfie taker.

Whether real, staged, or edited they are still important reminders to stop and look around before snapping that selfie.

Avoid dangerous selfies—most of us do not have the dexterity to take a selfie while dangling from a cliff with one hand.

Finally, do not take a selfie if it will compromise someone's privacy: in a bathroom, or a sneaky selfie with a celebrity.

Other than that, there is no wrong way to take a selfie; it is truly a reflection of yourself.

Take a selfie

Feel no shame

Start a selfie album

Malacoff, Julia. (2016, Sep 24). *Why Selfies Might Not Be Such a Bad Thing After All*. Retrieved from www.shape.com/lifestyle/mind-and-body/why-selfies-might-not-be-such-bad-thing-after-all

Themed Selfies

Earlier this year, I noticed I had taken quite a few selfies holding a bag of popcorn. Instead of being ashamed, I decided to make it 'a thing'.

I created a popcorn selfies album on Facebook, and now at every event I look for the popcorn.

Having a themed selfie allows me to look forward to an event, it motivates me to pay attention to my surroundings, and my friends are curious to see what popcorn selfie I will post next.

I also have wine selfies. Like the popcorn selfies, it was not intentional. I happened to attend a wine and painting class, a wine and sign (book signing), and drank some wine at a concert, and I took selfies on each occasion.

I'm not a big wine drinker so I started off taking the photos to show my friends: hey, I can drink something more sophisticated than soda.

Soon it became a thing, much rarer than the popcorn, but still a thing.

Figure out what your themed selfie will be. Some options are popcorn, pizza, snow cones, wine, free samples, a favorite food, tickets, fliers, souvenir collectible, event or movie posters, an event tee or hat, or other promo items.

Get creative with selfies and try different angles, different lighting, using mirrors, or taking barefoot selfies.

I love seeing those barefoot selfies where the feet are in the foreground and the mountains or beach in the background.

Themed selfies are memorable, unique, and just plain fun. They, like regular selfies, pull you into that moment and provide a chance to pause, breathe, and enjoy the moment.

Like regular selfies, it gives control to the photographer (you) and later on photos can be edited with frames, text, or stickers to make a personalized digital or print 'postcard' to go in a scrapbook or digital album.

Discover your personal theme

Take themed selfies

Embrace the happiness

Harless, Jennie. (2015, July 13). *15 Creative Selfie Ideas.* Retrieved from improvephotography.com/33394/15-creative-selfie-ideas/

Group Photos

I cannot count the times I have told people to get in the group photo.

Nevertheless, I still have those friends who stand outside the group or hide behind the tall people. I think it is fear that "the camera never lies" and people worry about their flaws standing out.

I get it. I really do. I had low self-esteem in my teen years and being in a photo is not something I would have jumped at twenty or thirty years ago.

However, group photos are the perfect way to get used to being in any photo, and to increase your esteem.

Group photos are usually taken at a distance, so most of what you want to hide, will be hidden. Additionally, being in a group photo just feels good.

It is an acceptance by society, a feeling of self-worth. For one moment in time, you and a bunch of strangers came together for a common purpose.

There was no fighting.

There were no biases or prejudices.

Everybody smiled and stood united for a common purpose: the group photo.

Group photos: the answer to World Peace.

Follow up with the photographer to find out how you can get a copy, or beforehand ask them to take a group photo with your camera.

I have been in photos for hiking, trail workdays, work related events, celebrations, contests, a wine-n-painting class, walking tours, creek clean-ups, and volunteer work.

Because I get in the group photo, I have ended up in various publications such as magazines, newspapers, websites, and newsletters.

As I was writing this book, my friend and her son were in a group photo for a cosplay contest (finally!)

The local newspaper printed the photo. After eight years of friendship, I finally was able to get her into the newspaper (my family and I are close to two dozen times in print).

However, she is in the back row—still hiding—and only part of her face shows. If you don't know to look, you wouldn't see her. No worries, she is still in training, but with me as her guide, she will learn.

Get in the group photo

Don't hide

Smile for the camera

Take lots of Pictures

It has become a game with my family to guess how many photos I take at events.

I'm so bad that I have reviewed events based on the amount of photos, "Oh it wasn't that great, I only took 60 photos."

At a charity event for work, I was designated photographer. In the first hour, the organizer turned to me and said, "Take more photos."

She did not see the artsy shots, the selfies, the group photos, the panoramas. Confused, I said, "I've taken 53, do you need more?"

Understand this; I come from an age without digital cameras. In fact, I come from an age of Polaroid cameras.

Aim. Click. Whir.

Thirty seconds later a print emerges. Two minutes later, an image shows up on the printout. If it did not look good, it was often too late to take another one.

Therefore, when the digital age emerged I became a complete photoholic photo hoarder.

I love taking pictures, but more so I love editing them. I have awesome photo editing apps on my phone.

People will say I take good photos, to which I reply: "I don't take good photos; I'm a good photo editor."

I also take multiple shots of one thing or scene in order to get the best one and I save all editing for when I am home.

Recently my brother and I had a small debate about taking photos. For one, he does not take a lot, and of those, he deletes the bad photos at that moment.

Not me, I edit when I get home, and I do this for several reasons: so I don't miss another photo opportunity while stuck in editing mode; to take my time editing later; and to relive the moment.

Of those 250 photos I take (not an exaggerated number), I might end up with 86 that are true keepers.

With all these photos, people might think I am hiding behind the camera and miss living in the moment.

I vehemently disagree.

This is not the age of camera operators hiding under a veil to snap the photo; this is not even the age of holding a camera to your face and mashing the viewfinder up against your eye.

With digital cameras, we are not viewing the world through a lens; we are holding the camera away from our face.

In fact, according to a study from Southern California and Yale University it was determined that taking a picture does not "pull you out of the moment" as normally perceived. It does just the opposite.

Taking pictures can heighten the enjoyment and helps us to remember more details and recall those details later.

However, keep in mind some basic etiquette as you shoot all those photos:

Respect it if someone doesn't want his or her photo taken.

Always ask a cosplayer, artist, vendor, author, or celebrity for permission first. In the cosplay world there is a saying "cosplay is not consent." If they refuse, respect that (in my experience, no one has refused a photo yet).

Turn off cameras (and cell phones in general) in the movies. Museums often do not allow photos of certain exhibits. Some live performance venues may not allow photos at all, especially flash photography.

When photos are not allowed, there are other ways to preserve the memories such as ticket stubs, pictures of the outside of the venue, programs and brochures, or souvenirs for purchase.

If photography is allowed, share it on social media and #hashtag the event, place, or person so that they can also see it, or post it to their Facebook page. Performers will enjoy seeing photos taken at their events.

Finally, keep it balanced. The secret to life is balance in everything you do. Make sure that you are not using photos to hide behind the lens to avoid interacting with others.

Put down that camera occasionally and interact in the scene.

And make sure you are in some of those photos.

Take lots of photos

Get in some of those photos

Edit at home

Barasch, Alixandra, PhD; Diehl, Kristin, PhD.; and Zauberman, PhD. (2016, June 9). *Take a Picture, You'll Enjoy It More.* Retrieved from www.apa.org/news/press/releases/2016/06/picture-enjoy.aspx

Photo Ops

Sometimes, there are photo opportunities in the way of green screens, photo booths with props, or tourist photos.

I have taken advantage of photo ops at Comicons such as a professional photo with *Soda City Photo*, a green screen with super-hero city added later, and photo booths with stick or real props (an amazing *Dr. Who* scarf about 20 feet long).

At a Titanic exhibit, I stood in front of a green screen and an image of the grand staircase was added later.

If there is a photo opportunity with props or in front of a screen, I will take it.

Photos ops like these can range from free (used as a promotional gimmick) to upwards of $20 for a tourist photo (like the Titanic photo). Always ask first if unsure of a price.

But, whether free or a fee, photo ops like these are memorable because you get a unique photo, often stamped with the location, event, or the date.

These photo ops take us out of the role of the photographer, and into the role of the subject.

It can also be a boost to the self-esteem to be the subject, especially when it is a professional photographer. They care about how their photos look since it reflects their business, so you will always look good.

It is also a great way to interact with the event; you step into the moment through a photo, and get a nice keepsake in the bargain.

Besides, it is just good old-fashioned fun to hold a mustache on a stick, drape a feather boa around your neck, or slip on that top hat. It is extremely difficult to take life seriously, worry about money, or be frustrated by life when you are holding a 'stache on a stick.

Be serious. Be silly. Do a solo photo, a couple's photo, a family photo, or a group photo with friends.

Take multiple poses, switch props often (when allowed), smile, and have fun. But, never miss an offered photo opportunity.

Look for the photo ops

Hold the fake mustache on a stick

Pose with the green screen

Food Photos

I know there are internet memes and posts that say food photos are annoying or pointless; after all, we do not show printed pictures of food to people in 'real life.'

I have two arguments about that:

1) This isn't real life, its social media and,

2) Yes we do.

I guarantee that in scrapbooks across the world are pictures of wedding and birthday cakes, banquets or potluck spreads, or steaks and burgers on the grill.

All of these have made it into someone's physical scrapbook or photo album, or shown to someone.

Granted, we are taking more food photos and food selfies than ever before, but it is the digital age and we are taking more photos than ever before.

When we were limited to 27 photos with disposable cameras or 24-36 photos with film cameras, we did not waste them on food photos.

Now we can take food photos. And lots of them.

I say people who do not like food photos are the same people against selfies. They are the ones who probably will not pick up this book. They are the ones who do not know how to make the most of each moment.

But, if I am mistaken and you *are* reading this book but still don't like food photos then you have my utmost, humblest of apologies—*now get out there and take a food photo!*

Food photos are a lot of fun...within reason. I am not going to take a picture of a burger and fries from

McDonalds...it is ordinary and plain. However, I might take a picture of a shrimp patty burger (Fillet-O-Ebi) from McDonalds in Japan, because it is different for me.

That amazing seafood spread, ethnic or cultural foods, an astoundingly giant pizza, or just anything that is a little different from your norm makes a good food photo

Not only do food photos make memorable moments, but also by sharing them, it might encourage others to try a new cuisine.

When taking a food photo, get creative with angles. Take a photo from your eye level, a bird's eye view, or level with the plate. Get a picture of the restaurant name, menu, or drink coaster in the photo, and when you can, go for the food selfie!

Take pictures of your food

Get the food selfie

Frame the restaurant name in the photo

Lee, Elynn. (2014, Aug 22). *Why Do People Take Pictures of Their Food?* Retrieved from www.quora.com/Why-do-people-take-pictures-of-their-food

Kiosks and Signs

Stop and take time to read the information on kiosks or signs. They are there for a reason, and might provide information that is not common knowledge or a tour guide might not mention.

Signs might be fun and silly, they might be educational, or they might be there for your safety. Either way, stop a moment and read the sign.

Because we are pausing the moment and learning something new, it can help solidify those moments in our memories, especially if someone reads the sign in their best movie-narrator voice like my daughter does.

Take pictures of the information kiosks signs, posters, and historical markers as well.

These photos can help identify a set of pictures in an album or file. Especially when visiting multiple places or visits spanning several days. They are good reminders of where a set of photos are from or give more information on the area.

Taking a picture of the sign helps you to remember the information and pulls you back into that moment, and the memories, when you re-read it in the photo.

Possibly, seeing pictures of information signs will encourage others to visit there...and that is a boon to local economy.

When possible, have fun with the sign.

One example for me is when I saw the sea level sign at Myrtle Beach State Park: One foot above sea level. I knew what photo I had to take.

Living in land-locked states most of my life I am still amazed and awed by the ocean and being this close to sea level. When I saw the sign, I begged my friend to stop a moment.

Raising my foot, I snapped a photo of it next to the sign. Later on, I added the text "You mean this foot?"

So stop, breathe, pause life for a moment and read or photograph the signs.

Stop and read the signs

Take a photo

Expand your mind

Be Creative

Need I remind my readers that this is the digital age. We can delete photos that are no good and take multiple photos without using up all the film in manual cameras.

Be silly. Be funny. Be creative and inventive. Don't stare at the camera with no smile like in the photos of the 1800's. We know in this day and time that cameras won't steal our soul...or if they do, we're already doomed.

So, have fun with your photos in both the taking of and editing processes.

For a concert by *The Barefoot Movement*, a bluegrass group that performs barefoot, I took a photo of my barefeet with their program and tickets in frame.

Take pictures of the s.w.a.g (stuff we all get) and mememtos when you get home by assembling them on a flat surface. In my house after a comicon event we now take Con s.w.a.g photos.

Take a selfie of you with the tickets or program brochure, or take a picture of these items held in the foreground with the stage or a scenery in the background.

Try different angles such as standing above or below the subject or getting a side view. Or, get people to pose in different ways in the photo.

We don't all have to stand stick-straight like the old couple in the *American Gothic* painting.

Borrowing from the background can also add a creative flair to photos. For example, if in a hunting lodge and there are antlers on the wall, try to get a picture so the antlers appear to be growing out of a person's head. Or, even though it is cliché, get the photo holding up the Leaning Tower of Pisa.

Creativity also comes in the editing process. Often plain and somewhat boring photos are made better when I edit. Have fun (but not at the expense of others) when editing.

At a recent Comicon I took a photo of my friend dressed as Jareth from the *Labyrinth* (Jim Henson, 1986) with Freddy Krueger from *A Nightmare on Elm Street* (Wes Craven, 1984).

I was a teenager when I saw both those movies. So, I added the text, "Jareth and Freddy: my teenage fantasy and nightmare in one photo."

Life is too serious, we need to pause it every now and then and have fun. Like a wise man once said, "Life moves by pretty fast, if you don't stop and look around every once in awhile, you could miss it." (*Ferris Bueller's Day Off*/John Hughes 1986).

Take s.w.a.g photos

Use the background in the photo

Think creatively

Videos and GIFs

When video cameras first became a household item back in the late 80's and early 90's we videotaped an entire event, instead of just pieces of it. But, cell phones make it so easy to take quick videos.

I take only short videos. This saves on the battery and helps to eliminate major editing to cut out scenes that are boring or inconsequential.

For example, my daughter led a hike for a National Trails Day at a local park. It was an hour-long hike. Instead of an hour-long piece of footage, I only took videos when she was talking about something.

Later, I looped these together and made a nice little video of her doing her thing in nature.

I also recently downloaded a GIF maker app and I am in love with it. I can take multiple shots with my cell phone and then loop these to make a GIF.

Videos can be uploaded directly to Facebook, but I find it is better to store them on You Tube. Not only do they reach a second audience but they are shareable to other sites.

Many people make video blogs, podcasts, or vlogs, to review or talk about an event they have attended which can generate revenue with ad placement or paid subscribers.

But, more importantly...they provide memorable moments.

Any form of media can enhance a person's perception by causing you to really look around and pay attention to the surroundings for lighting, backgrounds, and angles.

Additionally, it may encourage you to interact with people, attend various activities going on at the venue, learn a new skill, or participate in different activities in order to enhance the video's content.

Make a video

Create a vlog or podcast

Make a gif

Scrapbook

Now that you have all those photos, what to do with them?

Scrapbook!

Scrapbooking is a newer craft idea and is one of the neatest ways I know to preserve memories.

In the "old days", we put photos in a grid-like pattern in an album, and called it good. Now we scrapbook, and call them memories.

Scrapbooks today involve stickers, decorative brads, stamps, colored and patterned paper, paper frames, and so much more. A person could spend thousands of dollars on equipment and spend hours and hours scrapping.

However, to get started on a dime-budget, purchase colored or patterned computer paper, clear protective sheets, and a colorful 3-ring binder. Using double-side tape, tape runners, or glue sticks add photos, stickers and other embellishments.

Scrapping is very rewarding; it is leisurely and relaxing and brings back those memories. At events, you will find that you are more perceptive as you consider what photos to take and what s.w.a.g to grab for scrapbook layouts.

The best advice I can give for scrapbooking is to be creative and think outside the box. Search the internet for ideas and basic tips to get started, or attend a scrapbook class at a local crafts and hobby store.

And, now I'm going to contradict myself, sort of. Earlier I said take lots of pictures. However, do not scrapbook every picture.

Digital files and albums are the best places to store all of the pictures taken. Scrapbooks are for a few select ones.

An event can take up just a couple of pages, or special events can be an entire scrapbook.

Currently, I have scrapbooks for date nights, Comicons, and Bucket List items. Past scrapbooks have included camping or outdoor adventures, and of course family albums.

Photos saved to a flash drive, CD, or online storage, or storing prints in a photo file box allows a person to go back and scrapbook later too.

Embellishments come in many varieties so spend some time looking at craft and hobby stores, department stores, or any place that might sell regular stickers.

Create unique themed pages or albums through the photos and through the embellishments or patterned paper.

In addition to stickers and store-bought embellishments, add in business cards, a small flier, postcards, raffle tickets, wrist bracelets, or other flat mementos.

Digital scrapbooking apps and software with similar embellishments are another option.

Download editing apps to get access to frames, clipart, or captions to add to your photos.

There are numerous places to create digital photo albums such as Flikr, Facebook, or Instagram. Even department stores, such as Wal-Mart, have online albums that can shared or used to print photos.

Digital albums are nice because they are shareable on a variety of social media sites, allowing for family and friends far away to keep in touch and see what is going on.

Whether physical scrapbooks or digital, there isn't a much better way to preserve memories than in a scrapbook.

Buy a scrapbook

Collect mementos or stickers

Take an afternoon off and scrapbook

Actions speak louder than words

Try the Free Sample

I will try just about any food item once if it is a free sample served on a cracker or a toothpick.

I've sampled goat cheese, beer cheese, jalapeno & grape jelly, various breads, homemade grape juice, wine, lamb, trail mix, pickled watermelon rinds, foods of various ethnicities, desserts, and more.

If there is a free sample, I will sample it. Like the popcorn selfies, food sampling makes me more aware of my surroundings.

Instead of just doing a 'drive-by' of the vendor I will stop and actually look at what they have, pick up free promo items, grab a recipe card, connect with people, or learn something about the product, business, or service.

Trying the free samples also opens up a person's mind to a new food item or flavor. In some cases, it might open your mind to a culture or religion that you previously held stereotypes or misgivings about.

I attended an interfaith fair one year and each booth had free samples of a food corresponding to their religion or region. This encouraged people to communicate and interact.

It was also neat to taste the different spices or seasonings a culture uses, and to understand the foods important to that region or faith.

Free samples are also a great way to pause the moment and enjoy it.

It is a moment when you have stopped to take a 'breather' and you are using all your senses.

I know some people who never seem to go for the free sample. But, I have never gotten sick from a one and I don't know anyone who has and anyone with food allergies can always ask the vendor about ingredients.

So, get out there and try the free sample. If the food is exotic, bizarre, or just out of the norm take a food selfie or grab a recipe card if available.

Try the free sample

Savor the flavors and ask questions

Take a selfie with it

Hug the Mascot

This entry has come and gone, and come again. Just before publishing I added it back in.

I first added it when I hugged and took a photo with a mascot for a local electric company at an Earth Day event, but soon removed it. I just couldn't find a fit for it in this book.

I added it back in when I placed my arm around Smokey the Bear at a fishing and wildlife expo and realized it did deserve to be in here.

Partly because it is fun to take pictures with someone in costume, and partly because I love hugs.

It fills my little kid heart with joy to take a picture with somebody in a furry or cartoon suit. It appeals to me in a childhood innocence and nostalgic kind of way.

I haven't encountered anyone in costume yet who won't take a picture with an adult whether that is a mascot or someone in cosplay. It is sort of part and parcel for the job or the hobby.

However, always ask permission before taking that photo (especially of cosplayers) and if you do want to reach out for the hug ask permission.

Be kind and courteous...costumes can be hot and uncomfortable, there might be delicate pieces to the costume, or the person just might be tired from being in character all day.

But, mascot or cosplay photos can be just as thrilling as taking a photo with a real celebrity. The characterization is there, the enthusiasm is there, and photos with people in character or in costume will truly make for memorable moments and are great additions to a digital or print scrapbook.

Especially if you can find other things to go along with it. When I took the picture with Smokey the Bear, I received a bookmarker shaped like Smokey and a sticker that says, "I met Smokey."

They look great in my scrapbook.

So, when the opportunity rises...get a picture with the person in the furry bear costume or the woman in the princess dress and tiara.

And, when permission is granted...hug the mascot.

Photo ops with costumers

Be polite, courteous

Hug the mascot

Learn a Skill

During an event earlier in the year, I was reminded of an important lesson: never be afraid to try a new skill.

While visiting a farm day event I stopped at the Palmetto Tatter's Guild booth. A woman asked if I tatted and I told her no, that I was no good at it. She then asked if I had ever tried.

I had not, but assumed it was similar to crocheting, sewing, or knitting and I know I am not good at those.

First, I was informed that it is not similar to those other skills, and secondly she said I would never know if I didn't try. She said the only failed skill is one that is not attempted.

Then I was gifted a free tatted butterfly, about an inch big, as a reminder and encouragement to always try something new.

The butterfly, along with their business card, is in a scrapbook with a brief summarization of the story so that I will always remember to try something new.

Trying a new skill goes along with interacting. Often at vended events or in agricultural businesses there is a chance to try your hand at something new.

Don't be embarrassed. Don't feel shy. Don't worry about mistakes. The vendors are there to teach the skill, and they appreciate it when people try.

When I was younger, I was afraid to try something new or to participate in an activity because I was afraid of making mistakes and looking stupid.

I have overcome that.

Still, sometimes I forget or get too shy to interact or learn a new skill. At recent events, I didn't take the opportunity to sheer a sheep or shoot an 1800-style pistol. If I get the chance again, I will do both.

However, I have used a two-person saw to cut timber in a lumberjack camp and I have churned butter by hand at pioneer days.

At a survival day in a state park I made a belt out of an old tire tube, made a stove out of a can, made a spear from a tree branch, and made a lantern out of a soda can.

Sometimes we learn a one-time skill, just to see how someone else lives or feels. Sometimes it becomes a lifetime skill or hobby.

Either way, it is a great way to interact with and become part of the moment.

Learn a new skill

Show no fear

Make mistakes, it's okay

Get in the Conga Line

I was not able to go to a major Comicon in 2017 due to an illness, but I kept up with it via Facebook.

The thing I am disappointed in the most. Missing a Dead Pool conga line

I do not dance. But I want to dance. I want to get out there one day and rock the dance floor to everyone's amazement.

However, I think I am lacking the genetic code to do so.

I have tried belly dance, I have learned the Shag, and I have spun around the floor in various ballroom dances, I have even done the Time Warp. Nothing has stuck and I have not become an expert at any dance.

Nevertheless, I will "jump in the line" (Harry Belafonte, 1961) anytime. I have congaed, spiral danced, bunny hopped, danced with Native Americans, twisted ribbons around a Maypole, and stomped around at Oktoberfest.

I can do these dances because there is virtually no dance skill required. If you can walk, hop, skip, or kick your legs to music you can do a conga line.

Dancers simply move in a parade...like a soul train...rather than the horizontal line of a country line-dance.

There may or may not be handholding or hand-to-shoulder touching involved.

Similar to the group photo, there is a certain intimacy in having a shared experience and being close to strangers, putting aside all differences and biases for two minutes of fun.

Dancing in itself provides a social connection and acceptance of our peers. It is an ancient practice used to tell a story, appease the spirits or gods, to celebrate, or as a mating ritual. It is believed that our earliest ancestors practiced some sort of rhythmic dance.

Dancing at festivals fosters an appreciation for that culture or religion and can help to preserve cultural and heritage traditions, and to build rapport.

Dancing also relieves stress and is an excellent form of exercise. Even if it is only a two-minute line dance or ten-second Conga line, there are no adverse affects.

So, as the meme says, "dance like no one is watching." Trust me, they're not...they are too busy taking selfies, getting in the group photo, trying the free sample, or standing behind you kicking their legs in the Bunny Hop.

Get in the conga line

Start the conga line

Be the conga line

(Viewed 2017, June 22). *What Are the Benefits of Dancing?* Retrieved from www.benefitsof.org/what-are-the-benefits-of-dancing/

Get the Autograph

Comicons and book signings are excellent places to get autographed memorabilia. When you purchase a comic, photo, or novel ask for the autograph.

Artists, celebrities, and authors are generally always eager and willing to sign something, its good PR for them.

I love signing books and I never get tired of it. It shows that someone is interested in my work.

For the fan, it is a memorable moment because you often get a few seconds to converse with that person and get a few seconds of one-on-one time. Often they will offer a handshake or a heart-felt thank you.

Some autographs will be plain and simple, some have witty sayings, some personalize it with your name, and others are more elaborate.

My daughter received an autograph for a book she bought at a Comicon, and he spent a good while detailing the autograph with a gold calligraphy pen. No simple signature, but a piece of art in and of itself.

Sometimes the autograph might be on a t-shirt or event poster. My husband picked up a copy of the event poster for the *Sumter Comic and Fan Fest* in 2017 and asked the artist to sign it.

In the comic book world, artists often sell blank covers or comics with white areas for sketching. Not only does the customer get an autograph, but also they get to watch an artist at work and have a unique comic keepsake.

We have autographed books, prints, cards,

posters, comics, and photos in my house and each one is a cherished piece in our collection and in our home.

Ask for the autograph

Thank them for their time

Cherish the autograph

Enter Contests

Events and activities often have raffles, door prizes, or other contests. Enter them. Sometimes they are free; sometimes they cost only a few dollars with proceeds benefiting a charity.

However, nothing creates memories better than winning a prize, which also becomes memorabilia to add to a collection, a shadow box, or a treasure box.

Sometimes prizewinners have their photos taken for a publication such as a newspaper or newsletter, and this provides one more keepsake.

Additionally, if there is a contest prior to the event to win free tickets or VIP perks, enter it.

With the *Barefoot Movement* concert, I saw a contest to take a barefoot selfie and win tickets. I did and I won, so date night was free and I got bragging rights for winning.

I had not anticipated winning, I just thought it would be fun to take a barefoot selfie and post it to the Facebook page.

Just recently, I entered the birthday club with a local radio station. I just wanted to hear my name announced on the radio. But, they hold weekly and monthly contests.

By submitting my name, I was automatically entered into both, and I won the monthly drawing for a $250 gift card to a local furniture store.

There is a certain thrill at hearing a name or ticket number called, and the prize is an additional bonus.

Sometimes the contest is the adventure itself, such as costume contests. The experience alone is often worth the memories and if you win, it is just an added bonus and esteem booster.

If you do enter a contest, post a picture of you with the prize, the contest host, or of the venue and share it to their Facebook page along with a thank you.

It takes a lot of effort, time, and sometimes money, to organize a contest and they will be appreciative knowing you are appreciative.

Buy raffle tickets

Enter many contests

Be a good loser and a grateful winner

Tourism Challenges

My family knows I am addicted to tourism challenges (and I use that phrase for lack of anything better).

But, tourism challenges, or passport challenges, are a great way to interact and provide focus. They are like little bucket lists someone already wrote for you.

Typically, and each one can be different, there is a guidebook listing different locations or tasks to do at those locations. Visit a location and get that page stamped at kiosks or visitor's centers to win prizes.

I am currently working on the *Ultimate Outsider* program (visit all 47 South Carolina state parks, get a free T-shirt) and the *South Carolina Agritourism Passport* (visit agri-businesses for a variety of prizes).

Two years ago, my daughter and I completed the *Sumter County Passport* (visit twenty-two unique locations and win a prize).

I attended a large event one time that gave out maps of the vendors, and each vendor had a stamp. Visit at least ten of those vendors, get a stamp, and be eligible for prizes later.

There are broader ones, too, such as getting stamps from participating lighthouses through the Lighthouse Society (uslhs.org).

Some passport programs offer prizes and some are just for fun but the idea behind all of them is to get people active, and to explore the area.

They are also a boon to local economics as they can draw in tourist dollars.

For us (the tourist) it is fun, rewarding, and gives us a purpose when visiting somewhere.

Often, we connect as a society in chatrooms, Facebook groups, in person, or in clubs related to that challenge (the *Ultimate Outsider* program has an annual celebration).

Visit tourist, state and national park, or agri-business websites in your state or google "passport challenges".

If you cannot find any, then create your own and reward yourself in some fashion. Tourist challenges can be specific such as visiting all the lighthouses in South Carolina, or vague such as visiting 10 different Hard Rock Cafes.

I am currently on the quest to find 10 geocaches, and when I do, I will buy myself a geocache patch.

Keep a record of what you do and when you do it, take a picture or buy a postcard, and collect some memorabilia from each location.

Participate in a tourist challenge

Create your own challenges

Reap the rewards

Buy the T Shirt

A common souvenir gag line is "all I got was this lousy T-shirt!" Another saying to describe, metaphorically, that a person went through something is "Been there, done that, bought the T-shirt."

Both sayings have jokingly negative connotations; however, buying a T-shirt is actually a wonderful way to remember an event and becomes a great souvenir.

Ranging from $10 to maybe $25, tees are not a very expensive souvenir item and are more practical than a collectible piece, which sits on a shelf and collects dust.

Purchasing a T-shirt early, if possible, and wearing it to an event can help set the mood and put you in the right frame of mind for the event.

Tees purchased at an event become a wonderful souvenir because they have the location, date, and venue printed on them.

Tees can be worn as casual or sleep wear, they can be turned into pillows or quilts, and limited edition or signed tees can be mounted and framed.

When a movie comes out, buy a corresponding T-shirt and wear it to the theater. I wore a *Jaws* (Speilberg, 1975) t-shirt when I saw the movie projected outside on the side of a building.

When I saw Wonder Woman, I wore one of my many tees. Before I started cosplaying, I would wear tees with my favorite characters such as *Star Wars*, *Wonder Woman*, or the *Little Mermaid* to Comicons.

I also currently have tees for a Zombie Fest, a volunteer group, an eclipse viewing, movie tees, a tee shirt for a *Whoville* (Dr. Seuss) photo shoot, spirit week at work, the painted rock-hiding craze (*Kindness Rocks Project*, thekindnessrocksproject.com), a wrestler's tee, and more.

Eventually, I want someone to sew them into a T-shirt quilt for me, this will be a wonderful keepsake to show all of the things I have done.

Do not pass up a t-shirt just because of the old gag line. Tees are a great way to make each moment a memory.

Buy the tee

Wear the tee (at least once)

Save the tee

Cosplay

Cosplaying will help you to achieve many of the tips in this book: entering contests, group photos, learning a new skill, and possibly overcoming fears. It is also a freedom of expression.

If you like dressing up once a year for Halloween, then you should enjoy cosplaying.

Last year I was involved in a conversation regarding the struggles of costumes and someone said, "I'm glad people only dress up once a year."

Once a year? It is early in July as I write this and already I have dressed up seven times. Halloween is still three months away.

Cosplay (literally a contraction of 'costume play') is a lot of fun and can be as simple or as complex as you desire it to be.

I like simple, I like to be able to take off two or three pieces and be in "normal" clothes. Chances are that I am stopping somewhere before I get home, and I like to look somewhat normal.

My daughter and friend like to go all out, wear full costume, face makeup...and they will walk into any store like that.

I have not discovered any wrong way to cosplay, and characters do not have to exist only in comic books.

We have seen homemade and store bought, movie icons, celebrities, comic book and anime characters, originals, mashups, gender-swap costumes, cereal box icons, cartoon characters, and more.

Typically, Comicons are the venues, but it is not limited to that. We have cosplayed a pirate day, *Rocky Horror Picture Show*, *Pokémon Go* events, and special movie nights at the Sumter Opera House and Lexington Artists Commission (LAC) Gallery.

In fact, at the LAC, my friend and I were the only two in full cosplay and the organizer asked us to speak about our costumes and props. We were able to share our love of the movie and our photo ended up on the Facebook page.

Incidentally, if you are going to cosplay then enter the contests. When I was encouraging my daughter to enter I said, "Do it for the experience." She did, and since then she has won several prizes.

Maybe you win, maybe you don't. But you still stood on stage in front of people, you heard your name and character called, you received applause, and you showed off the thing or person you love.

Cosplay also gets you noticed, it generates compliments and photo ops, it is self-esteem boosting, and makes you a star for a day.

All of which are very memorable moments.

But, if cosplaying is really not your thing, go back to the previous entry and at least buy the tee shirt.

Cosplay

Enter the contest or parade

Take photos

Social Media

I am not as social media savvy as I could be, I stick with Facebook, Twitter and Pinterest, but social media is almost a necessity these days for interacting and sharing.

Following social media for a venue or an event keeps you up-to-date on schedules, parking, fees, or other pertinent information.

Social media also allows you to interact with event hosts or business owners as well as other followers.

If a website offers a newsletter, sign up for it to hear about events. Sometimes your photo might even end up in the newsletter.

If there is an event or venue that I attend and was not previously following on social media, I will make sure that I do so later on and I often share the page.

When the Sumter Opera House played the *Labyrinth* movie, I asked if it would be okay for us to cosplay for it.

Not only did they say yes but also their next post about the event said, "David Bowie inspired costumes encouraged." My question encouraged them to encourage others to dress up.

I connected with the Lexington Art Gallery on Facebook for another event, since it was a small venue and they knew we were an hour away and driving in sketchy weather, they held off starting the movie for us.

I often feel like I already know the people since I interacted with them on Facebook or other social media.

When at events quite often someone will say, "aren't you—?" and that is followed up with a thanks for sharing their page, a thanks for reviewing something, or a nice-to-meet-you.

Social media leads to internet networking as well as offline networking and can be very valuable to people trying to make a name for themselves or promote something. I have even made some very good friends through interacting with social media.

Following social media will generate ads for related items or events. Because of the *Labyrinth* movie at the Sumter Opera House and adding hashtags to posts, the *Labyrinth* movie at the Lexington Art Gallery showed up.

Comment, post, message, hashtag, follow, and share social media (without getting spammy or stalker-ish). It is the way of the world now and it is truly a wonderful way to connect, learn, share, and interact.

Follow social media

Interact with the social media

#Hashtag it

Variety is the spice of life

Save News Clippings

Quite often regional magazines or newspapers will have an article or ad about an event. I recently developed the habit of clipping these to save as scrapbook material (literally, cut-n-paste).

This started when I saw a beautiful ad for the Columbia City Ballet's rendition of *Beauty and the Beast* and I knew I would never capture a photo as good as that one.

I cut it out, and later scrapbooked it along with photos, the tickets, and the program. It looks great, and has it has the date and venue printed in the ad.

Now, when articles come out and it is something I think I will attend or am interested in, I will clip it and save it.

Not only does this give me scrapbook material or memorbilia for later, but its also readily availble if I wanted to look back on it for event details.

I keep the articles in a plastic box until after the event, and then scrapbook it along with whatever other mementos I have.

If, for some reason, you end up not going to an event then the article can be tossed in the recycling bin.

Newspaper or magazine clippings are wonderful not only because they provide the date, time, and place, but because there might be photos, historical information about the event or venue, or quotes from people involved.

Check newspapers prior to and after an event to look for articles. Don't forget to look up magainzes and newspapers online for printable articles.

When you are at an event, if the media asks for your photo or a quote, don't hesitate! Ending up in print media, either your words or a photo, is a great thrill.

I should know, my family and I have ended up in the local newspaper twenty-one times and magazines maybe a dozen times.

I always tell people to go for the interview. There is no better way to make a moment a memory than to be in an article about the event and get that one-on-one attention from the media.

Look for news clippings

Save the clippings

Scrapbook them or use in a collage

Souvenirs

Figure out what you want to collect and make that "your thing." That one thing you hunt for. Not only does it give you a memento to save in a shadow box or a treasure box but it also gives you focus.

I love embroidered patches and try to pick one up everywhere I go. If they don't have any, I will get a postcard or a sticker.

My friend and I have found some interesting and out-of-the-way places in my search to find the perfect souvenir item.

We stayed in Christianburg, Virginia when we went to St. Albans Asylum for a paranormal investigation.

I wanted to get some souvenir type items so we drove around and finally found Sellor's Old Time General Store: nostalgic soda, candy, gifts, and more.

Inside we saw Bacon-flavored everything including soda and sizzling candy, and a Bigfoot Research Kit, which I should have bought.

It is a very cute and entertaining store, I would love to go back, and we never would have stopped there if it were not for my quest to buy souvenirs.

However, collecting is not just a shopping experience.

Looking for souvenirs or collecting items builds observational skills and inspires creativity. Collecting can be nostalgic, a connection to the past, a token of achievement, or foster social connections by joining groups or fan clubs.

I know there are memes that say, "Collect memories, not things," but sometimes, collecting a thing *is* collecting a memory.

Our collections remind us of the places we went and that leads to memories of what occurred there or who was with us.

I attach my embroidered patches to my hiking daypack and I love to see a new one added. Each one is an achievement or a mark to show where I have been. It also opens up conversation when people see them.

We can collect both mementos and memories... as long as we balance it. So find that one thing you want to collect, and collect it.

Find your collectible

Collect it

Take a picture of it

Decker, Ed. (Viewed 2017, June 22). *8 Reasons Why Collecting Things You Love Is Good For Your Brain.* Retrieved from www.rewireme.com/insight/8-reasons-why-collecting-things-you-love-is-good-for-your-brain

Free Stuff

I am a temporary hoarder of all things free. I will grab the free magazines, cups, chip clips, magnets, pens, sanitizer, water bottles, pamphlets, brochures, maps, Frisbees, postcards, business cards, buttons, etc., etc., etc.

Every time I go to a vended event, I tell myself I will be selective in the free stuff I grab. Every time I go to a vended event, I grab whatever I see.

"Ooh, I want this. Oh, and this, and this...maybe this too...definitely need this," and so on until I am burdened with free junk.

Nevertheless, I love it. When I get home, I will sort through everything. Sometimes I keep what I collected, sometimes I give it away to someone else, and sometimes it becomes scrapbook material.

Collecting this free stuff brings you into the moment because you are showing an interest and pausing to look at things.

If you just walk around, glancing at each booth or vendor, you may miss what is for sale, or the information offered. Stop, listen to their sales pitch or story, grab some free stuff, and move onto the next.

By doing this you have paused and focused on just one vendor, rather than seeing just a span of canvased awnings or infinite tables.

Letting them talk their talk gives them practice in their story, informs you (and it might be just the thing you have been looking for), and it is just common courtesy to do so if you have stopped and snagged some s.w.ag.

Then, give a polite thank you and move on if there is nothing of further interest.

This does not mean you have to hit up every vendor, just visit the ones of interest to you.

Because I do this, it is often easier to remember a person, service, or business later on when I need something they offered.

So, collect the free promos, and when you get home and sort through it, don't forget to take a s.w.a.g photo.

Collect the free stuff

Listen to and thank the vendor

Take s.w.a.g photos

Buy Postcards

Hardly anyone mails letters or postcards in this electronic age, but postcards are the perfect souvenirs to send to others or to keep.

The act of collecting and studying postcards is *deltiology*, and along with stamp and coin collecting, it is one largest collectible hobbies, according to *The History of Postcards* website.

These little cardstock photos and cartoons are cheaper to mail than letters, do not require an envelope, and are among the cheapest souvenir item you can buy, typically ranging from .25 cents to $1 each depending on the size.

Postcards come in a wide variety such as funny, historical, scenic, informative, and religious, holidays, people, art, culture, local legends, and even recipes.

They have limited space to write and take up hardly any time to complete and mail. If possible, mail them from that location (hotels will often do this for you) so that the receiver has the postmark from that region (especially if an exotic locale).

In the book *Without Reservations: Travels of an Independent Woman* (Random House, 2012) the author, Alice Steinbech, traveled Europe on her own.

In her travels, she purchased postcards to mail to herself. On the back of each, she wrote a journal-style entry about the place or her experiences.

If I ever travel for any length of time, this is definitely something I would do. How exciting to get home and read mail from yourself, remembering places, experiences, and emotions you had forgotten about.

With the *Sumter Passport*, we ended up at an old general market and post office, the Lenoir store in Horatio, South Carolina (est. 1869).

With an old-time post office that looks like it is straight out of an old movie, and an odd and eclectic collection of old papers, memorabilia, and pharmacy bottles, the Lenoir store is almost a museum unto itself.

At each stop in the booklet, we wanted to do something so at the Lenoir store we purchased two postcards. One was mailed to my mom and I kept the other one to scrapbook.

Postcards can be that one item you collect, or in addition to other items.

Scrapbook them, mail them to friends, use them as dividers in photo file boxes, or add to backdrops of shadow boxes or a collage.

A person cannot go wrong purchasing a postcard as a souvenir.

Buy postcards

Mail to a pen pal, friend, or family

Keep one postcard for yourself

(Viewed 2017, June 22). *The History of Postcards.* Retrieved from www.emotionscards.com/museum/historyofpostcards.htm

Make a Collage

If you listened to the previous entries, there is now a hoard of photos, pamphlets, brochures, embroidered patches, postcards or other flat collectibles lying around the house.

Did you toss them all in a box to never to see daylight again?

Well, dig them back out and assemble them in a collage.

Yes, I mean the construction paper and paste collages we made as children.

Only upgraded.

Buy the backing (poster board, foam board, a bulletin board, or cardstock), buy an adhesive (tacky glue, craft glue, or hot glue), and purchase scrapbook embellishments.

Before gluing, assemble the items in a way that is appealing to the eye, shifting them around as needed. Trim photos, brochures, and postcards to fit or to trim undesirable parts.

Colored paper can be torn or cut with textured scissors to add different shapes and textures to the collage. Tissue paper, paper bags and scraps of wallpaper also add different textures and patterns.

Look through magazines for letters or words to add to the collage. Then glue everything on and when dry, get it mounted and framed.

Collages can be a theme, such as various beach trips, can display an entire year of fun, can show off just one adventure, or be a hodge-podge of various adventures.

Creating a collage is a great way to relive the memories at that time, and for years to come. It, along with scrapbooking, help to expand creativity and release stress after a long day.

Knowing you will make a collage later can also enhance your perception at an activity or event, as you will be more aware of what you are buying or picking up and how it will look in a collage.

Create a unique collage

Have it framed

Be perceptive

(Viewed 2017, July 7). "How to Make a Collage." Retrieved from www.wikihow.com/Make-A-Collage

Keepsake Boxes

A shadowbox is literally a 3D collage, and created in a similar process.

It is an enclosed frame with a glass front, similar to a picture frame only much deeper. Objects of various sizes and depth make for a pleasing and artistic display when framed behind glass.

Most craft or hobby stores sell shadow boxes in all shapes and sizes.

Gather small collectibles, both flat and three-dimensional pieces, such as shot glasses, shells, postcards, key chains, brochures, embroidered patches, or other items.

Lay all the items out in a design that you like and then glue or wire onto foam board and frame.

Add in the flat pieces such as business cards, brochures, fliers, or postcards you have collected.

Once framed and hung on the wall, it will be a great memory keepsake and conversation piece.

Memory boxes (I call them treasure boxes) can be of a more personal collection. Items that are meaningful to you but that you do not necessarily want glued into a shadow box or visibly on display.

I actually have one that looks like a treasure chest that my grandmother bought me in Mexico. It holds a variety of treasured items that, from time to time, I will pull back out and look at fondly.

Memory or treasure boxes are a more tactile way to hold collections. Remove an item to hold it, enjoy it, or read a treasured letter or postcard. Tactile experiences can trigger memories in a profound way.

Look for decorative boxes on one of your adventures, or shop thrift and antique stores for a unique box. Boxes can be any size or shape, come with locks, and be as plain or as decorative as desired.

Craft and hobby stores often have plain wooden or cardboard boxes to decorate—another great project to foster creativity!

Shadow or memory boxes are also great gifts to give to someone who shared an adventure with you, or to hold that one item you have decided to collect.

Sort your collectibles

Frame items in a shadow box

Create a memory box

Journal It

I have many journals: a Happiness Journal that I write funny moments, quotes, or add stickers too.

I have a One-Sentence a Day Journal in which every day for five years I write one sentence summarizing the day.

And, I have a Bucket List Journal that I write about all the things I crossed off my bucket list.

Scrapbooking can also be considered a pictorial journal.

Journaling is an excellent way to make each moment a memory. Like some of the other tips in this book, it makes you more aware of your surroundings as you try to remember everything to write about later.

It will open your mind, clarify thinking, help you to process what you said and did, and it can increase creativity. Writing in a journal can also help a person connect with their feelings.

By starting a journal you will notice what things are important to you—what things make you happy or sad. Having this connection to your inner self and can make for a happier you with a much-improved esteem.

You may realize what things need to be filtered out of your life, or which things you need to do more of to improve your quality of life.

Journals will also help to solidify the important things, the intangible things, as you are likely to write more about conversations, people, and feelings rather than things purchased.

There are numerous decorative and themed journals for sale on the internet, bookstores, and department stores. But, a blank notebook, or loose leaf paper in a three-ring binder works just as well.

Make entries stylish and unique with colored pens to draw doodles or sketches, or add stickers. Star stickers for rating an event 1-5 is another idea.

Title each entry such as *Florence Comicon*, or get creative and flashy like a newspaper headline: *Super Hero's Invade the Midlands!*

Don't forget to include the date, venue name, and location. At the end of the year, or even years later, go back, read the journal, and reminisce about each moment.

Journal it

Add stickers

Use colored pens

Hyatt, Michael. (Viewed 2017, September 7). "The 7 Benefits of Keeping a Daily Journal." Retrieved from michaelhyatt.com/daily-journal.html

When in Rome, do as the Romans do

Be a Tourist

Where can you get all the collectibles, postcards, and pamphlets I have been urging you to collect?

Be a typical tourist and stop at visitor and welcome centers, gift shops, or nature centers and museums.

Not only are they great stops for collectibles, but employees and volunteers can often tell you more about the area you are visiting and recommend hotels, entertainment, or restaurants.

Visitor's Centers and Welcome Centers are usually near landmarks, state borders, highly visited tourist stops, or near historical points of interest.

Often, they act as a wayside rest along highways and interstates for travelers to stop and stretch their legs, use bathroom facilities, or get something to eat.

Visitor's Centers will often have souvenir items, free brochures, stickers, and maps and there are often photo opportunities, such as signs or face cutout boards (Virginia, whose motto is "Virginia is for lovers" has the giant letters of L-O-V-E).

Gift shops are the obvious choice for collectibles and souvenirs, but not every town has a gift shop, or it may be just a smaller section inside of another facility.

If you ever get to Myrtle Beach, I highly recommend visiting the gift shop the Gay Dolphin on Ocean Boulevard (www.gaydolphin.com); it is an experience unto itself.

Gift shops often are thematic to their region. For example, at the ocean the items for sale will be nautical themes, shells, and starfish. In the desert, it will be rain sticks, scorpion paperweights, and gag gift rattlesnake eggs.

State and National parks often have nature centers with gift shops, free tourist information, interactive activities, and family-friendly educational or fun programs.

Lynches River County Park just outside of Florence, SC is one of the best nature centers I have seen with looped video reels, a working microscope; animal print castings (the Grizzly Bear will give you nightmares); building blocks; interactive quiz; and a variety of other hands-on activities.

Hunting Island State Park has a nice nature center that includes pictures for identifying marine life and a display of shark's teeth, a lighthouse museum, video reels, and there is a nice gift shop on the island.

Museums often have gift shops too; there may also be family-friendly programs, and interactive activities. With so many different kinds of museums, visiting them can become a bucket list item or become the adventure itself.

I have visited a cotton museum, button museum, lighthouse museum, state museum, pioneer museum, two different war/military Museums, and a Lizard Man museum (local legend).

Google museums, state parks, national parks, visitor's centers, or nature centers for the area you are planning to travel in. Don't forget to spend some time in your own state or county exploring these different tourist stops. It is a great way to learn more about your community and to connect with it.

Tourist stops can really enhance the experience and memories by what they offer, and may even *become* the adventure themselves.

Visit tourist shops or centers

Buy collectibles

Attend a program or event

Write a Bucket List

Someone once said to me, "You're too young to have a bucket list." This statement makes no sense to me. How can a person be too young to have a list of things they want to do in life?

Granted, I am not old or at the end of my life, but I could die at 100 years old, or I could die tomorrow. Either way, I want to have lived. If I have to wait until I am dying to live, well that makes no sense.

Besides, I have revised the definition of bucket list. Instead of things to do before I kick the bucket (which is a negative connotation), it is a list of things to *fill* my bucket: Bucket of life, bucket of my soul, or a bucket of happiness...whatever you call it, fill it.

I read a poem in high school about the bucket and the dipper. We all have an esteem level called our bucket. When you get a compliment, the dipper adds water (good feelings) to your bucket. When someone is mean, the dipper takes out water.

The point of the poem, or at least the meaning I got, is to leave someone's bucket fuller than it was when you met him or her.

However, we can fill our own bucket by doing things that are enjoyable to us.

Creating a bucket list is easy. Get a tablet and write down all the things you want to do. Add to it often.

Bucket list journals are available online, but I recommend my own *Apocalist: the Bucket List with an Apocalypse Twist.* It is a standard bucket list but apocalyptic themed.

In the book *Bucket List Journal: Create a Lifetime of Inspiration and Purpose* (Rock Point Publishing, 2015) by Alex Wagman he mentions why a bucket list is important.

Having one gives you an enthusiasm for life, makes goals manageable, helps you to focus on what you want in life, helps you to discover your full potential, and it brings happiness.

I know bucket lists give me focus and I look forward to going to a certain place or event if I can cross something off my list. Often bucket list items lead me to other things I didn't even know I wanted to do.

A bucket list is like a set of goals or challenges, but usually in a fun way. Sure, it can have "lose ten pounds" on it, but I keep those goals or resolutions separate from my bucket list. A bucket list is not what I *need to do*, but what I *want to do*.

At the time of writing this book, I was looking in the July 2017 issue of *Parade Magazine* and it had an article titled *Happiness Boosters*. One of the items was "have a bucket list buddy."

The article stated that according to the *Journal of Personality and Social Psychology*, devoting time to different experiences can bring us happiness and those experiences are even better when shared with someone.

I am lucky enough to have a bucket list buddy and often I will tell her "we need to plan an adventure, I want to cross something off my bucket list."

So create that list and have fun with it. Items can be small such as trying a new restaurant or big, like visiting another country.

Add or take away items as needed. Often our desires, wants, and needs change. If an item no longer appeals to you then take it off the list.

Remember, a bucket list is a list of things we *want to do*. If that item becomes something you *have to do*, it becomes a chore and will not fill your bucket.

As you cross items off the bucket list, remember to collect photos, selfies, or memorabilia and journal or blog about it.

And, remember to take along a bucket list buddy.

Write a bucket list

Do the bucket list

Find a bucket list buddy

Cristol, Hope. (2017, July 9). *Living to 100: Happiness Boosters*. Retrieved from /parade.com/584686/hopecristol/get-happy-with-these-8-happiness-boosters/

Embrace the Culture

When in Rome, do as the Romans.

I tell people that growing up in a small town (700 people) has made me fascinated with other cultures and religions as an adult. Lack of exposure to these things has caused an overdose now.

When I meet someone from another culture or country, I just want to sit, listen, and absorb everything said.

At one state park event, I met two women from England, and it is one of my favorite conversations in memory.

We went back and forth on the differences in the countries with road travel, country size, cultural diversity, foods, and we dispelled (or confirmed) rumors of each other's country.

I have a cousin that converted to the Muslim faith and I love to connect with her and learn about her beliefs, as well as learn how she combines Kurdish food with American food (she is a culinary genius and one day I hope to sit at her table).

My daughter has a friend whose parents are from Romania and Hungary, and I love getting into conversations with them, learning the language, and hope to dine at their table too.

I love to learn and embrace other cultures, religions, and traditions. But just because I do, I am not being disloyal to my own country or beliefs.

I am learning and becoming open-minded.

Embracing a culture, or at least taking the time to learn a little bit about it, can cause open-mindedness, acceptance, and diminish judgments, biases, or prejudices.

When we achieve that, we bring our world a little closer, and when we achieve that we help to dispel the misconceptions and stereotypes others hold.

Take time to talk to others, put aside your pre-judged notions or biases and stereotypes. Whether that culture is religion, another country, a lifestyle, or just going to another state. Be open-minded and immerse yourself in that culture.

If something does go against personal or spiritual beliefs it is okay to refuse politely, but stay open-minded and do not judge others.

Rather than just observe, or ignore, the customs and traditions of a region, culture, or religion embrace them for that moment. Learn something new. Make that moment memorable.

Learn about another culture

Respect that culture

Diminish fears and prejudices

(Viewed 2017, June 22). *How to Respect Other Cultures.* Retrieved from www.wikihow.com/Respect-Other-Cultures

Make the Old New

Pokemon Go, geocaching, passport or tourist challenges, and the *Kindness Rocks Project* (thekindnessrocksproject.com) have made familiar and "old" places new again by exploring them in a different way.

That same old park you have visited a hundred times takes on a new meaning when there are Pokemon to catch, rocks to hunt for, or a stamp to collect.

By revisiting familiar places we can make different memories instead of blurring them all together.

For example, if you always walk the same path and let the kids play on the playground at a familiar park, then all those moments blur together.

But if you go and walk the same path hunting for rocks or Pokemon then it creates a unique memory.

Now, we know that *Pokemon Go* will not be around forever, and that tourist challenges or rock-hunting might not be available in an area or may be fads that die out.

So, when necessary, create your own theme or challenge for visiting an old place. Plus, creating a theme or challenge can be a wonderful bonding time with family or friends as you all sit down and try to figure out what to do and where.

Talk with as many people as you can, take along someone new, go with the intention of writing an article or making a video, or take artistic photos.

See an old familiar movie in a new venue or attend a new event in a familiar place (main street looks different when decorated with zombies and Halloween costumes).

Little things like these allow you to see a familiar haunt with new eyes and will not only create more memories at favorite venues, but will make each moment more memorable.

Re-visit something familiar

See it through new eyes

Make different memories

Immerse Yourself

To make a moment memorable, immerse yourself fully into that moment: Attend multiple events on a related theme or create other memories of that event throughout the year.

It is sort of like "psyching" yourself into it. Setting the mood, if you will.

Prior to pirate day at the beach my friend and I shared pirate videos on Facebook. On the way to the beach, we listened to the soundtrack for *Pirates of the Caribbean* (Disney/Bruckheimer, 2003).

Anytime we go to *The Labyrinth* we listen to the soundtrack for it, and we cosplay the characters.

When the release of the live-action *Beauty and the Beast* (Disney, 2017), I also attended the Columbia City Ballet who did a rendition of the tale, and I bought a full-color mini-poster book from the movie.

When the release of *Wonder Woman* (DC Entertainment, 2017) I read a graphic novel, the novel adapted from the movie, and cosplayed the character.

In 2012, the 100th anniversary of the sinking of the *Titanic* (James Cameron, 1996), I dressed as Rose for Halloween, saw the remastered 3D re-release, and saw the Titanic exhibit at the state museum.

With the Solar Eclipse in 2017, a local assisted-living facility was offering moon and sun themed snacks such as Sun Chips ™ and Moon Pies ™.

When the Kindness Rocks project took off in my county, I attended two rock-painting events, joined Facebook groups, and spent several days hiding and painting rocks.

Buy that superhero t-shirt and wear it to the movie. Read the book or comics. Cosplay a character at a Comicon. Listen to a soundtrack before the movie.

Having a year, or even a month, of *Titanic*, of *Labyrinth*, of *Wonder Woman* is more memorable than a one-time experience. It also broadens horizons, creativity, and perspective.

If it is not possible to do multiple things for a specific topic that is okay. You can still go 'all in' and fully immerse yourself in that one moment.

When I saw *Sixteen Candles* (Hughes, 1984) at the Sumter Opera House I dressed 80's for it and listened to the music on the way to the movie.

For the Jaws movie not only did I wear the shirt, I also ate gummy shark candy, and painted a rock for the venue owner that said "I watched *Jaws* and survived."

Incidentally, that year became a year of seeing movies in obscure places: an opera house, art gallery, and in a parking lot of a pharmacy.

I bought movie themed stickers and embellishments and scrapbooked about all the different venues I saw movies in that year.

To find multiple events or venues, connect with people on social media, post or review events, search for similar events using key phrases, and hashtag key words.

Another option is to create your own theme. For example, make summer the season of visiting state parks, or this a year of museums. Attend as many holiday related events as you can.

Other options are to cross off as many bucket list items as you can or visit five (or more) new places.

With a little thought, prep, and planning you can make your own adventures that will not only be fun but also geared to your own specific tastes and interests as well as creating memorable moments.

Wear the t-shirt

Listen to the soundtrack

Read the book

All Five Senses

In this book, I mention many different ways to make each moment a memory some of which utilize different senses such as interacting (touch), and trying the free samples (taste).

However, I wanted to create an entry just for our senses, as we often take them for granted.

I do not have to think about the sheep's wool for my fingers to feel the texture. I do not have to think to taste a free sample. Our eyes, ears, and nose automatically pick up sights, sounds and smells.

We need to stop and focus on our senses focus on what they are experiencing, and learn to use as many senses as we can in one experience.

In touching the sheep's wool, notice the somewhat rough texture of the wool, but also notice the oily texture of the lanolin in it. Is there a smell to it? What does the wool look like?

When wandering around a large venue look for individualism: see the people, the costumes, the vendors, or the displays.

Search for that collectible item or photo opportunity. Focus on and commit to your memory the colors, textures, and patterns surrounding you.

Listen to sounds: music, conversations, laughter. If outdoors listen to nature, not music from a radio, I guarantee nature will provide its own symphony.

Be an attentive listener and really hear the words said, or let the music of a concert touch your soul.

When allowed, pet the animals; touch the

snakeskin; feel the fabrics (never touch artwork, the oils in our hands can be very damaging).

Feel the different textures and take note of them. Think about what it is you are touching and how it makes you feel (safe and comfortable, or leery and uncomfortable).

Tasting is a sense we do not always observe, often eating meals just to stave off hunger or provide nourishment. However, eating is not just nourishment for the body but for the soul.

When dining, focus on the food: the textures, aromas, sight, and tastes. Taste the free sample offered. Taste can trigger a memory as easily as anything else can.

The taste of apple butter reminds me of my childhood fortress: a crabapple tree. I staged my first (and only) protest in that tree when dad said he was cutting it.

(Turns out, he only wanted to trim limbs away from a power line, but I still consider it a win.)

The sense of smell is often ignored, unless it is a strong aroma. Sure, we all remember movie theaters when we smell buttered popcorn, and fried foods remind us of the county fair.

But smell can trigger memories and heighten emotions sometimes more effectively than other senses, according to the *Fifth Sense* website.

Pay attention to other smells, and not just the strong ones that jump out at us instinctively.

By consciously using our senses and paying attention to each one, we can heighten our memories, broaden our observations and perceptions, and remember those moments easier in the days to come.

Savor your food

Smell the roses

Touch what you can

Listen attentively

Observe life

Birds of a feather, flock together

Single-Serve Friends

I have often told my girls that some friends come into your life for only a little while and some stay for a lifetime.

Two different media formats have recently helped confirm this, and put the sentiment in better words than I could.

Again, in Steinbech's book *Without Reservations,* she mentions a time at a crowded Parisian Café when a woman asks to join her at a table. A non-fiction book, Steinbech mentions that sharing a table is the best way to meet people when traveling.

She further states that sometimes a real, and lasting, friendship can grow out of such encounters but she says that most often it is a "temporary friendship, one rooted in the mutual need of two strangers to find companionship in unfamiliar surroundings."

In the movie *Fight Club* (Fincher, 1999) the term "single-serve friends" is used to refer to a person who is your friend for a short-period of time.

I fell in love with that term: single-serve friend.

It doesn't mean that the single-serve friend is any less important than the lifelong friend. It just means that they were there when you needed a friend at that time.

A good example is my daughter at a Junior Ranger camp in 4th grade. She made friends with a girl from out-of-state staying with her grandmother for the summer. The girls bonded over a pile of mud, and were the best of friends that week.

Each of them knew they had a field trip buddy, a lunch buddy, and someone to share the experience with.

Sometimes we don't even know the names of our single-serve friends, but that doesn't dimish their importance.

While camping one year, we were near a family that participted in many of the same events that weekend, we even shared a campfire.

The following year I saw them at Hunting Island State Park. A year after that, we saw them on a trolley when we participated in the *Sumter Passport* challenge.

Not knowing their names we called them 'that family' and immediately we'd know who we were talking about. It seems we saw them at least once a year and they are fondly stuck in our memories.

I often think of them as single-serve friends because we don't hang out, we don't see each other on a regular basis. But, we recognize each other, stop and chit-chat, and exclaim over the growth of our children (in their case, adding children to the brood).

I also know they are a loving family, adventurous, and they know how to make the most of each moment.

I don't know if we'll ever get to the point of long-term friends, or if they remain as "that family" that I bump into on ocassion when out adventuring.

Either way is fine with me, they are a delightful family and seeing them brings a smile to my face.

In my opinion, single-serve friends are special in a way that lifelong friends can never be.

Lifelong friends are always there, we enjoy the same things, laugh or cry at the same things—that's why we're friends. We know why we are friends, when we became friends, and that we will always be friends.

But to bond with a stranger for a week or a day—to find someone on your same level of weirdness in a mass of strangers on such quick notice? Now, that's special.

Keep your mind open to single-serve friends, and cherish the moments with them. Take a selfie with them, connect with them on social media, share a table together.

Single-serve friends shared a common experience with you, they bonded with you, and they connected with you. It is a form of social acceptance and a boost to the self esteem to make a friend so quickly.

Hopefully they appreciate you as a single-serve friend just as much as you appreciate them.

Cherish a single-serve friend

Take a selfie with them

Connect on social media

Bring a Friend

Bringing a friend is a great way to make each moment memorable.

It's someone to reminisce with later. It's someone to take pictures with. Someone to laugh with. Someone to stick your head through a photo cut-out with. Someone to hold an extra stick prop when you grabbed too many.

I have an amazing friend that when I call, post, or text "hey...do you wanna..." she says "yes." She is my go-to-gal and our motto has become "if you're driving, then I'm riding."

There hasn't been anything we've come up with that the other one has not agreed to.

We always have a great time and we push each other to try new things, face our fears, or challenge ourselves.

That's probably the best thing about bringing a friend. There's one person who understands you and knows your limits, yet will encourage you when you try to push those limits.

She's the one who spent the night with me on a fishing pier; she's the one who encouraged me to walk the rope bridges at Lynches River County Park. She's the one who is encouraging me to go back to a lighthouse and make it to the top.

I've taught her about hiking and encouraged her to walks seven miles of hiking trails—twice! I'm the one who spent the night with her in a haunted asylum. I'm the one who eventually got her picture in magazines and the newspaper.

We love to do different things, and we are always trying to encourage our family and friends to join us. We joke that we need a party bus for our adventures.

Sharing experiences gives one a good feeling. It's nice to surround yourself with positive people and to share an experience with them.

It is nice to have someone along that understands you, enjoys what you enjoy, and someone to appreciate the moment as much as you do.

Bring a friend

Share the memories

Live, laugh, love

Go it Solo

If there isn't someone to go with you, or it is something you'd rather do on your own, there is no harm in going solo. An event can be just as enjoyable when alone as with others.

It took me years to get comfortable with that. I never wanted to go anywhere alone, I feared being pitied, "Oh, poor dear, no one likes her."

Now, I realize that people aren't thinking that. And, those who do think it, they aren't worth my time.

The biggest reward in going solo is in knowing that you have the confidence and esteem to do it!

Another advantage is that there won't be any distractions. You will be left alone to your thoughts to enjoy wherever you are without extra conversation, bathroom breaks, or complaints.

Going it alone can help you to utilize all of your senses as mentioned earlier. When others are distracting you it is more difficult to focus on our senses, possibly just taking them for granted.

There are actually a few things I prefer to do alone. Recently, the Opera House showed the movie *Ferris Beuller's Day Off* (Hughes, 1986). I did not tell anyone *not* to go, but it eventually ended up that I went alone.

But, it was a good thing. I had wanted to attend it alone anyway for very psychological reasons.

I was in my teens when the movie first came out, and I saw it alone.

When I moved from my hometown to the other side of the country, I watched Ferris every day, sometimes twice a day—rewinding it and watching it back-to-back (last count, I was up to twenty-four viewing times).   All those times I watched it alone.

Those three characters became my friends and made me feel good at times when I didn't. They loved each other for who they were and they truly knew how to make the most of each moment. I always wanted friends like that.

So, when it was showing at the Opera House I had wanted to watch it alone. However, not because I don't have good friends, but because I do.

It was a final nod to the movie, a type of closure perhaps. I watched it when I hadn't friends, and now I can watch it knowing that I do have those friends

Watching it solo showed me how far I have come. I have friends like Cameron, Ferris, and Sloane, and I am also comfortable enough to go it alone.

 Life has brought me from feeling lonely and scared to try anything new, to a place where it is now possible for me to jump in a parade, eat at a fine restaurant, visit an art gallery, or take in a ball game.

Going solo is a great accomplishment, but if it is something you are still not comfortable with, take baby steps. Dine-in at a fast food restaurant instead of a five-star. Go the park and take a walk instead of attending an event alone. Go to the movie theater instead of seeing a live performance.

These places are less conspicuous and will get you used to doing things and going places alone.

Once you are comfortable with that it won't be a struggle to attend other events or go other places solo, and you will be amazed at how good you will feel.

The down side to going solo? No one to supervise you. I recently went to an outdoor concert solo because no one else could make it. Turns out, later on my husband was able to come out for a short while.

But, by the time he got there I was deep into a Mango Daquiri poured into a real pineapple.

Why? Because I had never had a drink in a pineapple before. That was all the reason I needed.

And the little umbrella will make a great scrapbook embellishment!

Go it solo

Boost your self-esteem

Don't worry what others think

Talk to People

I used to by shy. When I tell people that, they laugh and tell me to stop 'storying'. But I was. No lie. I didn't voice an opinion, I didn't express a thought, I didn't talk to new people.

Now, I'll talk to anyone anytime and for any reason.

Getting into a conversation with someone is memorable because it is a connection with someone new. It is a connection in this sea of people with different personalities, different backgrounds, and different beliefs.

To connect with someone briefly is amazing and can lead to lifelong friendships, single-serve friends, or just a memorable conversation.

Recently, as I was leaving a local festival, we we saw a business offering free snowcones.

Well, try the free sample, right?

So, we each got a free snowcone (and took a snowcone selfie) and I commented on how good it was. The gentleman replied "thanks, we only use the freshest ice."

Not missing a beat, I asked "oh? Is it a family secret then?" and he came back with "no, not so secret. Just water and lots of cold stuff."

We both laughed at our hilarity and he wished us a good day. The best part of this conversation is that the two people with us made no comment, as if they are used to such inanity from the company they keep.

I love to get in conversations with people. I like to learn about who they are and where they are from. Everyone is unique and has a unique personaility.

We are all individuals and we should learn about each other and take the time to listen to what others have to say (even if we don't agree) and to be open to what they might teach us.

Remember my earlier example with the tatting booth? I was reminded to try new things, and was gifted a tatted butterfly, all because I engaged in conversation.

If we all see each other as people and not stereotypes then I think the world can be a happier, more peaceful place, and maybe the conversations will *become* the memorable moment.

Start a conversation

Listen attentively

Respond

Share Memories

Throughout this book I have mentioned several ways to share memories through digital albums, articles and reviews, and social media.

This isn't to brag or make others envious.

(Well, maybe a little...who doesn't want to brag about eating gummy sharks while watching *Jaws*?)

Sharing is important mainly because sharing memories is food for the soul.

Telling stories draws us together as a people, it helps us to laugh, to cry, and to bond. Reminiscing can fill us with good thoughts and feelings.

Sharing also helps to make a moment memorable because it is relived in that moment.

Sharing a funny memory—a silly photo or themed selfie—might be the one thing that brings a smile to someone having a bad day.

Family and friends can keep up with what you are doing and feel a closer connection. I know that with this long-distance family I have, sharing memories of things we've done helps us all to feel closer.

Sharing your memories might also encourage someone to visit the same place you have, which can promote tourism in your town or favorite place.

Another positive to sharing our memories is that when others see them, it might encourage them to branch out of their comfort zones and try something new, or it might teach them how to make each moment a memory.

So, go ahead, share those albums, tell those stories, brag about the adventure, teach someone else a skill you learned, and show others how they can make each memory a moment.

Share the memory

Brag about an adventure

Encourage others to do the same

There is no time like the present

Be a Good Listener

Most of us probably think we are good listeners. Most of us would be wrong.

It is important to be a good listener, to hear what a person is saying, and be able to retain it or retell it later.

This does not mean we have to repeat it verbatim, but we should be able to retain, paraphrase, and retell what has been said or learned.

We should be able to understand and comprehend what the speaker is trying to convey. To ask questions that are meaningful and on-topic.

Attend your full concentration and attention on the speaker. Let them complete their sentence or story before interrupting. Then, when an interruption is necessary, do so politely and with purpose.

Not only is it polite to attentively listen to someone, but we can gain so much from what it is said or how it is said than if we are distracted or interrupt often.

We need to actively listen, and not be passive listeners.

Passive listening is letting the speaker talk but not really focusing on the words. Instead, our minds wander to what we are cooking for dinner that night or to that business meeting coming up.

However, actively listening means empathizing and sympathizing with the speaker; understanding, and comprehending what the speaker is trying to convey.

Only then will we become good listeners and by

doing so, we are making the moment more enjoyable not just for ourselves but for everyone around us.

In a world where we are multi-tasking seemingly every second of the day, a conversation is one of the few places we should stop multi-tasking and focus on only one thing.

By listening to someone, actively listening to them, we may make that single-serve or lifelong friend, we will learn a little more about the event or venue, and we can retain the memories a little bit better because we have cleared our mind temporarily and were focused.

Actively listen

Focus on the content

Interrupt as little as possible

Ask Questions

We first learn by asking questions but as adults, we tend to forget or feel self-conscious at asking them.

Asking questions is still how we learn and knowing you are going to ask questions later will make for more active listening.

We can learn a lot about others or our surroundings if we ask questions, whether the setting is a general conversation or a question and answer venue.

When asking a question, do so with intent and interrupt politely. If a speaker asked to hold all questions to the end, do so but write down questions so you will not forget.

Questions should also be on-topic and not used to embarrass or harm someone. Ask with sincerity, to clarify, or to learn.

When you ask a question, apply the active listening skills learned earlier. Hear the answer and respond appropriately or thank the person for answering.

It is no use to ask a question and then start scrolling through your phone or otherwise divert your attention. You asked the question, so listen for the answer.

Plan your questions so you know exactly what you want to ask and focus questions on one thing at a time.

By asking questions, we first actively listened to the speaker and we received follow-up information.

This makes for a more memorable moment because we were focused and in that moment for that duration. Our memories will be able to retain it better because of the interaction.

Ask questions

Interrupt politely and purposefully

Listen to the answer

(Viewed 2017, July 25). *Ten Tips for Asking Good Questions.* Retrieved from www.dummies.com/careers/find-a-job/interviews/ten-tips-for-asking-good-questions

Face Your Fears

Within reason. I state again, within reason.

Everyone should know his or her limits. Whether those fears stem from very real concerns, or the phobias of unknown origins we all seem to have.

Know your limits but do not let fears debilitate you from life.

If it is a fear of bridges, have someone else drive or find an alternate route, rather than avoiding the place completely.

If terrified of dolls, don't visit the doll museum, but don't let it stop you from visiting other museums.

Some fears are even challengeable, if taken in small steps. It does not mean you will overcome the fear, it just means for this one moment you conquered it—and this makes for a very memorable moment!

I am afraid of drowning. Not water itself, just of drowning. My quirks with water are very weird and often it depends on who I am with or the circumstances.

I have walked on docks and piers, but only if they are wide enough and stable enough. I will go into natural bodies of water, but not very far and never in a boat. I will go in a swimming pool, but never on a floaty (too tipsy).

That being said, In 2016 I slept overnight on a fishing pier at Myrtle Beach State Park.

But I almost didn't.

As soon as my foot took the first step on the pier, I regretted my decision. It was longer and higher up than I thought. We could feel it swaying.

We decided to stick it out as long as possible because there were other programs and events involved and I had paid $60 for us to be there.

If nothing else, we decided we would stick around for the other programs, and then leave when it was time to camp out.

However, by staying we learned that we were not restricted to sleeping at the far end of the pier. We could sleep anywhere along it, or we could go to our cars. We could hang out on the deck at the visitor's center, and we didn't even have to sleep.

I was able to set my limits. Which meant we were close to shore. But, the challenge was to sleep on a pier overnight with no shelter.

Challenge accepted and met!

I also bought an embroidered patch depicting the pier to show off my newfound bravado.

Fear can limit our full potential. It is very inhibiting and can cause depression, loss of enthusiasm, and stop us from doing things we might otherwise enjoy.

As a child, I didn't do a lot of things. My fears stemmed mainly from a lack of self esteem and confidence.

However, as an adult I am more willing to try different things.

My motto has recently become "as a child, I was afraid to try new things, as an adult I am afraid not to try new things."

When we are afraid of what others will say or think, we might never sing that song, give that lecture, or write that book. Who knows where any of those things might have led us?

Fear of certain things can stop us from enjoying a moment or engaging in something new. Fear can also drain us emotionally and mentally.

However, conquering a fear can lead to positive feelings and increase in self-esteem.

Set your limits, and face your fears.

Set limits

Face your fears

Brag about your bravado

Breathe In, Breathe Out

Now, after telling you to interact, learn a new skill, take lots of pictures and selfies, and read the signs I'm going to contradict myself and tell you to stop.

But just for a moment.

Stop everything you're doing, or about to do, and just pause life for a few seconds. Breathe in. Breathe out. Enjoy the moment without the clutter of other thoughts or actions.

Reflect on where you are and what you are doing: standing on the ocean's shores; the top balcony of a lighthouse; or you just learned how to milk a cow.

Breathe in. Wow. You did it. Think about what led to this moment, how you got here, or that you finally got here.

Deep breathing eases stress and tension and will make you more comfortable and relaxed in that moment, which will aid in better recollecting that memory later.

This pause in life will also help you to take it all in, to really appreciate the moment and to give your body a chance to stop distraction and to utilize all your senses. Focus on each one and take mental note of what you feel, see, hear, taste, and smell.

Life is busy and hectic and if we are not thinking ten thousand things we are mutlki-tasking ten-thousands things.

Take that little moment, thirty seconds or so, to just push the pause button on the remote control of life and breathe in, breathe out.

Clean your mind and just enjoy the moment. Your body, mind, and soul will be grateful that you did and you will help to solidify that moment in your memory bank as you absorbed each moment of it without committing to anything else at that time.

Breathe in

Pause and reflect

Breathe out

Random Moments

This entry came in late in this book. It was not one of the originals, but after visiting a quaint thrift store titled Grandma's Attic on highway 441 in South Carolina, I realized I needed an entry for it.

I was not expecting this to be a memorable moment, although the store—with its many nooks and crannies, rooms, and layers upon layers of stuff—is memorable in and of itself enough.

When I got to the counter, I picked up a business card. At the very least, I was going to blog about it. Next to the business card, I noticed three typed poems on cardstock about the same size as the business card.

I picked one up and the owner said, "Those are poems I wrote. They're free." I have never received free poems at a store before and the poems are actually very good. It was unexpected, but very pleasing.

I scrapbooked all three poems with the business card in my "inspirational" scrapbook. I took a selfie in and outside the store to add to my Facebook blog.

Another time, at work for Mother's Day, our male co-workers bought red roses and each female received one.

Of course, I took a selfie with my rose, and placed it in my animated *Beauty and the Beast* mug (Disney, 1991) in my office.

I learned years ago to look for these random and unexpected moments and to enjoy them when they come up. Not every moment has to be a long vacation, an annual event, or in a large venue.

Sometimes the random or little events are the best and most important.

Always carry a camera (smart phones are great for this). Carry a tablet and a pen to write stuff down. Keep your mind open and look for the unexpected moments.

Do not think about dinner tonight, do not think about the bills you have to pay, and do not think about how life is letting you down.

Instead, think of the fact that someone took the time to give you a flower at work. Appreciate that free meal. Enjoy those free poems. Pause, breathe, cherish that moment and be grateful.

Those little memories will last you a long time. Often when a failure at life mood creeps in, it is those small moments that get us through.

Appreciate the random

Pause, breathe, smile

Enjoy the unexpected

Combine Tips

I've already shown a few ways how the tips in the this book can be combined.

In one entry I mention getting a free snow cone which falls under talking to someone, getting the free sample, and themed selfies.

At a Zombie street dance, I dressed in costume, talked with people, and took lots of photos.

On the fishing pier I made single-serving friends, faced my fears, learned about a new culture, and engaged in conversations.

Many of these things just happen and come naturally, but by being aware of them you will make that moment more memorable.

As I said in the intro: don't do every tip every time. That would cause too much stress, defeating the purpose, and isn't even feasible. But, it is possible to do many of the tips in here at one event.

For example: a carnival is the perfect place to take a selfie, take a themed selfie, find photo ops (cardboard cutouts or stick props), try a free sample, and maybe make a single-serve friend.

This doesn't mean force yourself to go out and do each of these things. We are not working on a "to-do" list. It merely means to be open to these possibilities.

If you see a photo booth with stick props, take a photo. If someone is offering free samples, take a bite. Be open to a good conversation with someone.

When we know to look for opportunities, such as in this book, we will find that they will start to find us. This book is to teach you to not avoid those opportunities, and when possible to make a few opportunities for yourself.

When the opportunities come up, do as many of the things as you can that will help make each moment a memory.

Before you know it, each moment will become a memory and you will enjoy each thing you do just a little bit more.

Look for memorable opportunities

Take advantage of the opportunities

Make the moments memorable

Live in the Moment

It can be difficult to live in the present moment, but it is necessary for your well-being.

Living in the moment does not mean you are ignoring the future or forgetting the past, and above all else, it is *not* permanent.

We can live in the moment by not worrying about the future (temporarily) or regretting the past by stopping, breathing, and just living in that moment for a little while.

It is often easy to live in the moment when we are watching a movie or reading a book, the words and scenes take our minds to a different place.

However, if we are simply observing, wandering around, or listening to a conversation our minds tend to drift. When this happens, pull yourself back to that moment by snapping that selfie, trying that free sample, or talking to others.

When you are in a moment, whether at a Comicon, attending a quilting bee, or wandering around the county fair, do that one thing. In an age of multi-tasking, we need to step back and single task occasionally.

When I am at an event, I am *at that* event, not somewhere in the past. Conversation is what is occurring at that event.

I am not balancing my checkbook or paying bills while wandering around the fair or community festival.

I am not making appointments while watching a movie.

I am not catching up on letter writing while I am hiking a state park trail.

I am enjoying each single moment as it comes up. Appreciating who I am with—friends and strangers alike—appreciating the common cause and interest.

I am attentively listening, asking questions, taking photos, collecting memorabilia.

It might take practice, but it is achievable by doing what's mentioned in this book, and it is worth it.

To live in that moment is truly the best way to make each moment a memory.

Pause time

Live in the moment

Make each moment a memory

Author Bio

Deanna Anderson is a mom, a wife, and an author who resides with her family in Sumter, South Carolina.

Some of her memorable moments include sleeping on a fishing pier for a public camp-out and walking a wildflower labyrinth. She enjoys wearing costumes for events, takes selfies, always gets in the group photo, and collects embroidered patches, postcards, stickers, and other oddities.

In addition to independent publishing, she writes freelance for local publications like The Sumter Item, Lakeside Magazine, Sumter Living and has written as a guest blogger for Let's Go! SC.

She is interested in attending events, doing podcasts, hosting book signings, or guest blogging and would love to hear from her readers or anyone interested in having her at an event.

Email her at deanna.anderson.author@gmail.com.

www.amazon.com/author/deannaanderson

Other Titles

Fiction Titles
Twisted Worlds
(Formerly Retorta Mundis: Twisted Worlds)

Themed Journals
Success Journal
Hiking Journal
The Apocalist

New Age
Magick for the Elemental Witch
365 Tarot Activities
My Tarot Journal

Now all nine titles in **Twisted Worlds** are
available as individual Kindle editions! Search
author's name, book title, or short story title.